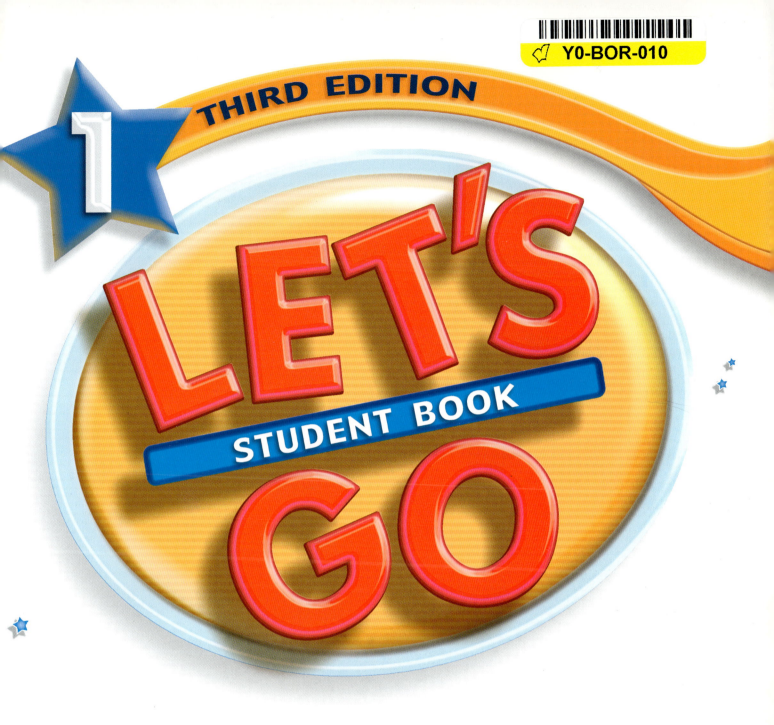

Let's Go
STUDENT BOOK
THIRD EDITION 1

Ritsuko Nakata

Karen Frazier

Barbara Hoskins

with songs and chants by Carolyn Graham

OXFORD
UNIVERSITY PRESS

OXFORD
UNIVERSITY PRESS

198 Madison Avenue
New York, NY 10016 USA

Great Clarendon Street, Oxford OX2 6DP UK

Oxford University Press is a department of the University of Oxford.
It furthers the University's objective of excellence in research, scholarship,
and education by publishing worldwide in

Oxford   New York

Auckland   Cape Town   Dar es Salaam   Hong Kong   Karachi
Kuala Lumpur   Madrid   Melbourne   Mexico City   Nairobi
New Delhi   Shanghai   Taipei   Toronto

With offices in

Argentina   Austria   Brazil   Chile   Czech Republic   France   Greece
Guatemala   Hungary   Italy   Japan   Poland   Portugal   Singapore
South Korea   Switzerland   Thailand   Turkey   Ukraine   Vietnam

OXFORD and OXFORD ENGLISH are registered trademarks of
Oxford University Press

© Oxford University Press 2006

Database right Oxford University Press (maker)

No unauthorized photocopying

All rights reserved. No part of this publication may be reproduced,
stored in a retrieval system, or transmitted, in any form or by any means,
without the prior permission in writing of Oxford University Press,
or as expressly permitted by law, or under terms agreed with the appropriate
copyright clearance organization. Enquiries concerning reproduction outside
the scope of the above should be sent to the ELT Rights Department, Oxford
University Press, at the address above.

You must not circulate this book in any other binding or cover
and you must impose this same condition on any acquirer.

Any websites referred to in this publication are in the public domain and
their addresses are provided by Oxford University Press for information only.
Oxford University Press disclaims any responsibility for the content.

Editorial Manager: Nancy Leonhardt
Senior Editor: Paul Phillips
Associate Editor: Geof Knight
Art Director: Maj-Britt Hagsted
Design Project Manager: Amelia L. Carling
Designers: Jaclyn Smith, Alicia Dorn
Art Editor: Judi DeSouter
Production Manager: Shanta Persaud
Production Controller: Zai Jawat Ali

ISBN-13: 978 0 19 4394390   STUDENT BOOK
ISBN-10: 0 19 4394395   STUDENT BOOK
ISBN-13: 978 0 19 4394321   STUDENT BOOK WITH CD-ROM (PACK)
ISBN-10: 0 19 4394328   STUDENT BOOK WITH CD-ROM (PACK)
ISBN-13: 978 0 19 4395571   CD-ROM
ISBN-10: 0 19 439557-X   CD-ROM

Printed in Hong Kong

10 9 8 7 6 5 4 3 2 1

ACKNOWLEDGMENTS

To our editors at Oxford University Press, and to the design team, thank you for your creativity and hard work. To our husbands and children, thank you for your support, understanding, and willingness to eat fast food. We would like to dedicate the series to the many teachers and students who have crossed our paths over the years. You have been our inspiration.

Illustrators: Zina Saunders: 2, 3, 5, 10, 11, 13, 20, 21, 28, 29, 30, 36, 37, 38, 39, 46, 47, 56, 57, 64, 65; Janet Skiles: 4, 6, 8, 12, 14, 16, 17, 18, 22, 24, 26, 30, 32, 34, 35, 37, 40, 42, 44, 48, 50, 52, 53, 58, 60, 62, 63, 66, 67, 68, 70; Chris Reed: 17, 23, 26, 53, 59, 72; Terri & Joe Chicko/Cornell & McCarthy: 4, 24, 45, 68; Sharon Harmer: 44, 52, 72; Steve Henry/Cornell & McCarthy: 16, 22, 36, 50, 60, 63, 72; Kevin Brown: 6, 9, 18, 41, 54, 61; Priscilla Burris/Chris Tugeau: 23, 26, 33, 44, 49, 67; Richard Kolding: 16, 18, 34, 37, 52, 63, 71; Jane Smith: 17, 58, 62, 70, 72; Brenda Sexton: 27, 42, 48; Christine Schneider/Maggie Byer-Sprinzeles: 11, 40, 43, 57; Liz Goulet Dubois/Maggie Byer-Sprinzeles: 7, 25, 33, 53, 55; Susie Lee Jin: 15, 29, 45, 71; Ann Iosa: 9, 51, 54, 59, 69; Mindy Pierce/Chris Tugeau: 8, 31, 34, 43, 47, 65, 70, 73; Nelle Davis/Craven Design Studios: 25, 54, 62, 72; Patrick Girouard/Portfolio Solutions: 36, 41, 73

Cover illustrations by Zina Saunders and Janet Skiles.

Table of Contents

Unit 1 Things for School	page 2
Unit 2 Colors and Shapes	page 10
Units 1–2 Listen and Review	page 18
Let's Learn About Numbers 0–20	page 19
Unit 3 At the Store	page 20
Unit 4 People at Home	page 28
Units 3–4 Listen and Review	page 36
Let's Learn About Parts of the Body	page 37
Unit 5 Birthday and Toys	page 38
Unit 6 Outdoors	page 44
Units 5–6 Listen and Review	page 54
Let's Learn About Days of the Week	page 55
Unit 7 Food	page 56
Unit 8 Animals	page 64
Units 7–8 Listen and Review	page 72
Let's Learn About Feelings	page 73

Hi, I'm Ginger.

Hi, I'm Sam.

Icons

Let's Start

Let's Build

Let's Learn

Units Review

Let's Learn More

Let's Learn About

Unit 1 Things for School

 Let's Start

A. Let's talk. (CD 1 / 02)

 (CD 1 / 03)

What's your name?
My name is Kate.

What is = What's
I am = I'm

B. Let's sing.

The Hello Song

Hello, hello, hello!
　What's your name?
Hello, hello, hello!
　My name is Scott.
　My name is Scott.
Hello, Scott!
Hello, Scott!
　Hello!

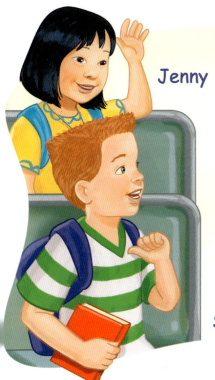

Jenny

Scott

Kate

Andy

C. Let's move.

1. stand up

2. sit down

3. make a circle

4. make a line

Let's **stand up.**

A. Practice the words.

1. a pencil

2. a pen

3. a bag

4. a book

5. a desk

6. a chair

7. a ruler

8. an eraser

B. Practice the sentence.

It's a pencil.
It's an eraser.

It is = It's

4   Unit 1 / Things for School

C. Practice the question and answer.

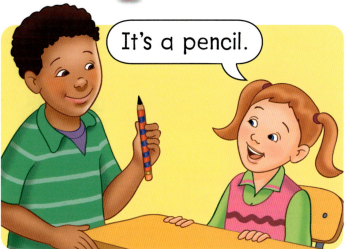

Let's Learn More

A. Practice the words. 🔊 CD 1 14

1. a map

2. a marker

3. a globe

4. a table

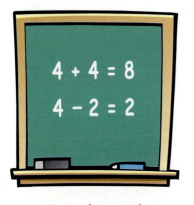

5. a board

6. a wastebasket

7. a poster

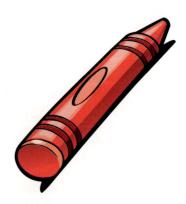

8. a crayon

B. Practice the sentence. 🔊 CD 1 15

This is a map.

6   Unit 1 / Things for School

C. Practice the question and answer.

Is this a table?
   Yes, it is.
Is this a crayon?
   No, it isn't. It's a marker.

is not = isn't
It is = It's

D. Ask and answer.

1. Is this a book?

2. Is this a book?

Unit 1 / Things for School   7

Let's Build

A. Learn the alphabet and sing.

The Alphabet Song

B. Practice.

1.
2.
3.
4.

C. Listen and circle.

1.
   a　　　　　　b

2.
   a　　　　　　b

3.
   a　　　　　　b

4.
   a　　　　　　b

D. Ask your partner.

1.　　2.　　3.　　4.　　5.　　6.

Unit 2 Colors and Shapes

 **Let's Start**

A. Let's talk. CD 1 24

CD 1 25

How are you?
　I'm fine. Thank you.

I am = I'm

B. Let's sing.

Hi! How Are You?
Hi, how are you?
I'm fine.
Hi, how are you?
I'm fine.
Hi, how are you?
I'm fine. How are you?
I'm fine, I'm fine, I'm fine.

fine   great   OK

C. Let's move.

1. take out your book

2. put away your book

3. draw a picture

4. point to the poster

Please take out your book.
Take out your book, please.

Unit 2 / Colors and Shapes   11

Let's Learn

A. Practice the words.

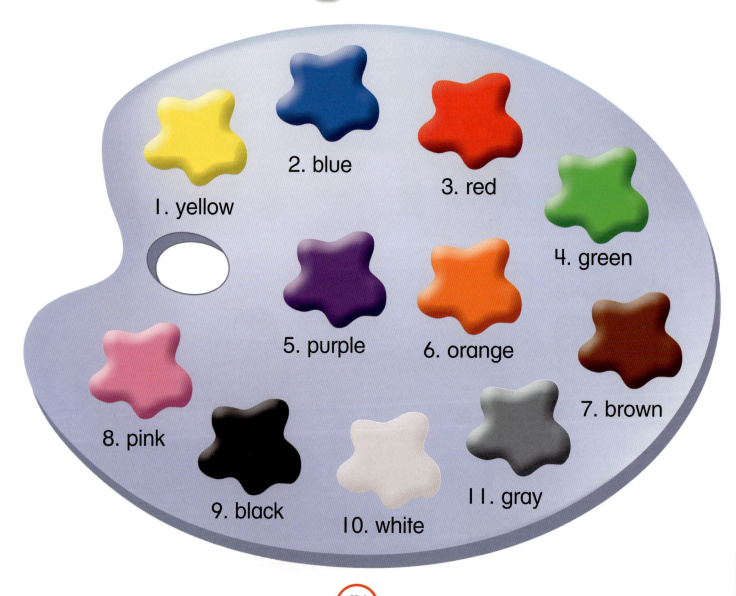

1. yellow
2. blue
3. red
4. green
5. purple
6. orange
7. brown
8. pink
9. black
10. white
11. gray

B. Practice the sentence.

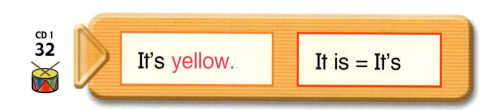

It's yellow.   It is = It's

Let's Learn More

A. Practice the words. (CD 1, 37)

1. a triangle

2. a square

3. a circle

4. a star

5. a heart

6. a rectangle

7. a diamond

8. an oval

B. Practice the sentence. (CD 1, 38)

This is a triangle.
This is an oval.

Unit 2 / Colors and Shapes

C. Practice the question and answer.

Is this a star?
  Yes, it is.
Is this a circle?
  No, it isn't. It's an oval.

is not = isn't
It is = It's

D. Answer the question.

Is this _____?

1. a square? | 2. a circle? | 3.  purple? | 4. ☆ a star? | 5.  green?

Unit 2 / Colors and Shapes 15

Let's Build

A. Practice the alphabet.

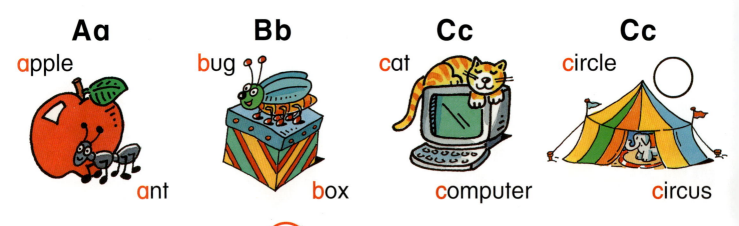

Aa — apple, ant
Bb — bug, box
Cc — cat, computer
Cc — circle, circus

B. Ask and answer.

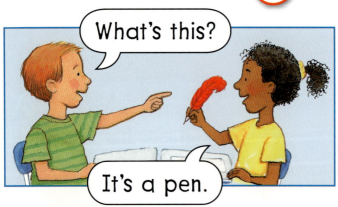

1.
2.
3.
4.

What's this?
   It's a pen.
What color is it?
   It's red. It's a red pen.

16   Unit 2 / Colors and Shapes

C. Practice.

D. Listen and sing.

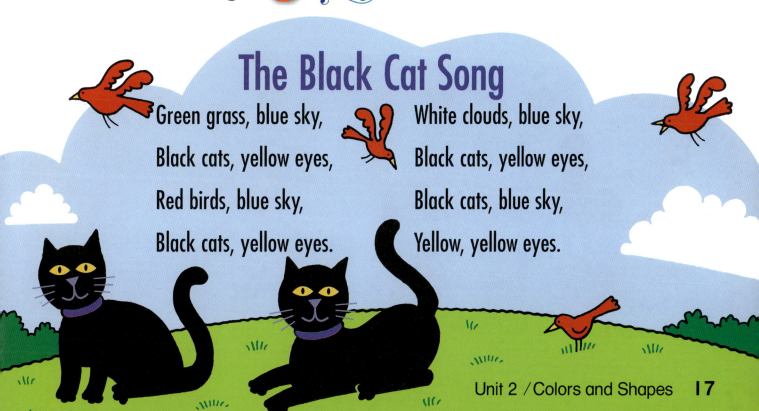

The Black Cat Song

Green grass, blue sky,
Black cats, yellow eyes,
Red birds, blue sky,
Black cats, yellow eyes.

White clouds, blue sky,
Black cats, yellow eyes,
Black cats, blue sky,
Yellow, yellow eyes.

Units 1–2 Listen and Review

A. Listen and circle.

1.
a b c

2.
a b c

3.
a b c

4.
a b c

5.
a b c

6.
a b c

7.
a b

8.
a b

Let's Learn About Numbers 0-20

A. Count to ten. (CD 1, 48)

0 zero

1 one

2 two

3 three

4 four

5 five

6 six

7 seven

8 eight

9 nine

10 ten

B. Count to twenty. (CD 1, 49)

11 eleven

12 twelve

13 thirteen

14 fourteen

15 fifteen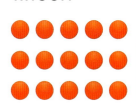

16 sixteen

17 seventeen

18 eighteen

19 nineteen

20 twenty

Unit 3　At the Store

 Let's Start

A. Let's talk.

  This is my friend, Sarah.
Hello, Sarah.

B. Let's sing.

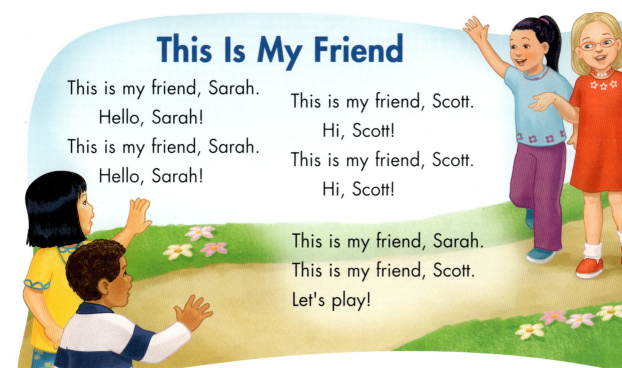

This Is My Friend

This is my friend, Sarah.
Hello, Sarah!
This is my friend, Sarah.
Hello, Sarah!

This is my friend, Scott.
Hi, Scott!
This is my friend, Scott.
Hi, Scott!

This is my friend, Sarah.
This is my friend, Scott.
Let's play!

C. Let's move.

1. count to ten

2. write the word

3. read a book

4. say the alphabet

I can count to ten.

Let's Learn

"How many crayons?" "Three crayons."

A. Practice the words. CD 1 56

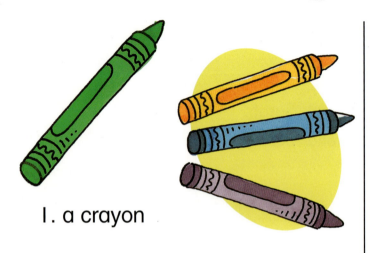

1. a crayon
2. crayons

3. a marker
4. markers

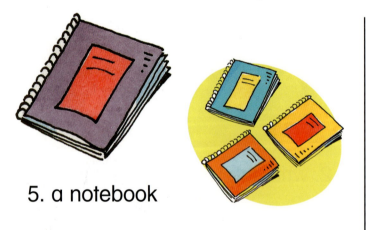

5. a notebook
6. notebooks

7. a pencil case
8. pencil cases

B. Practice the sentence. CD 1 57

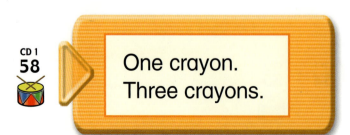

CD 1 58

One crayon.
Three crayons.

22   Unit 3 / At the Store

C. Practice the question and answer.

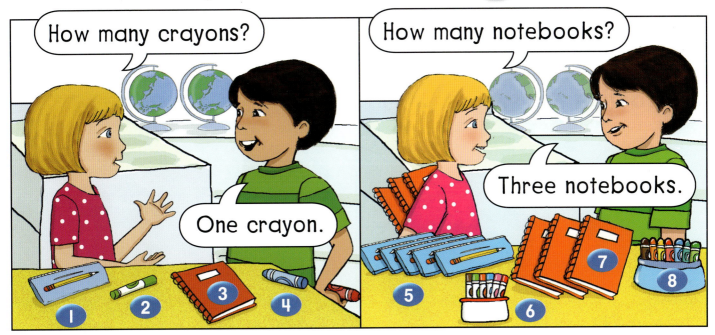

| How many crayons? | How many notebooks? |
| One crayon. | Three notebooks. |

D. Listen and write, then sing.

How Many?

Crayons, markers, pencil case, pencil case.

Crayons, markers, pencil case, pencil case.

2 crayons, ___ markers, ___ purple pencil case.

How many crayons? ___ crayons.

How many markers? ___ markers.

How many purple pencil cases? ___ purple pencil case.

Unit 3 / At the Store 23

What are these? They're CDs.

Let's Learn More

A. Practice the words.

1. a CD

2. CDs

3. a video game

4. video games

5. a cell phone

6. cell phones

7. a computer

8. computers

B. Practice the sentence.

It's a CD.
They're CDs.

It is = It's
They are = They're

24 Unit 3 / At the Store

C. Practice the question and answer.

What's this?
   It's a cell phone.
What are these?
   They're video games.

It is = It's
They are = They're

D. Ask and answer.

What is this?   What are these?

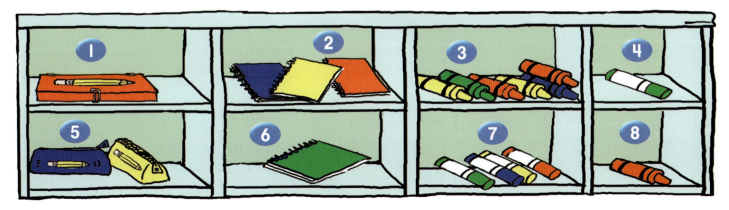

Unit 3 / At the Store   25

Let's Build

A. Practice the alphabet.

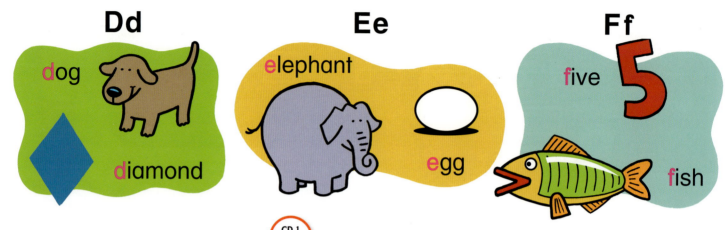

B. Ask and answer.

C. Ask your partner.

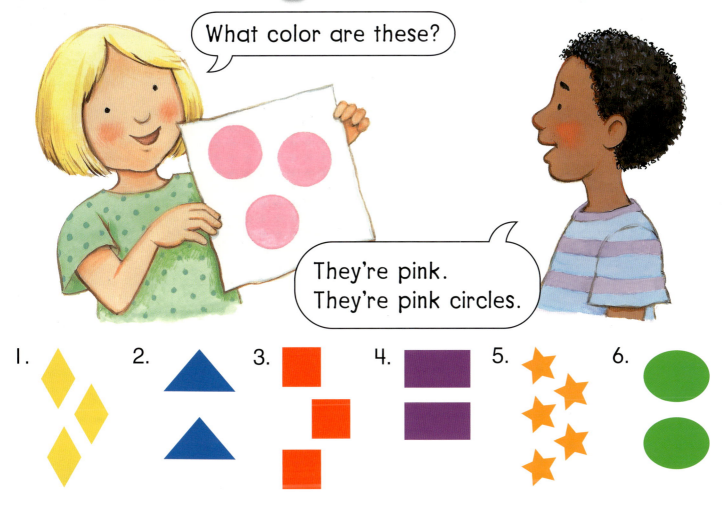

1. 2. 3. 4. 5. 6.

D. Listen and sing.

What's This?

What's this?
    It's a blue CD.
What's this?
    It's a red CD.
What are these?
    They're green CDs.
How many CDs?
    Ten!

Unit 4 People at Home

Let's Start

A. Let's talk.

It's nice to meet you.
It's nice to meet you, too.

It is = It's

B. Let's sing.

The Family Song

This is my mother.
  Nice to meet you.
    Nice to meet you, too.
This is my father.
  Nice to meet you.
    Nice to meet you, too.

This is my sister.
  Nice to meet you.
    Nice to meet you, too.
This is my brother.
  Nice to meet you.
    Nice to meet you, too.

C. Let's move.

1. find my book

2. reach the bookshelf

3. see the board

4. hear the teacher

I can find my book.
I can't find my book.

cannot = can't

Unit 4 / People at Home 29

Let's Learn

Who's she?
She's my mother.

A. Practice the words. CD 1 79

1. grandmother
2. mother
3. sister
4. baby sister
5. grandfather
6. father
7. brother

B. Practice the sentence. CD 1 80

CD 1 81

She's my grandmother.
He's my grandfather.

She is = She's
He is = He's

C. Practice the question and answer.

Who's she?
　She's my sister.
Who's he?
　He's my brother.

Who is = Who's
She is = She's
He is = He's

He's tall.

She's short.

Let's Learn More

A. Practice the words.

1. tall

2. short

3. young

4. old

5. pretty

6. ugly

7. thin

8. fat

B. Practice the sentence.

He's tall.
She's short.

He is = He's
She is = She's

C. Practice the question and answer.

Is he short?
   Yes, he is.
   No, he isn't. He's tall.

is not = isn't
He is = He's

D. Listen and circle, then sing.

Is He Short? Is He Tall?

Is he short?	Yes	No	Is she tall?	Yes	No
Is he tall?	Yes	No	Is she short?	Yes	No
Is he young?	Yes	No	Is she old?	Yes	No
Is he old?	Yes	No	Is she young?	Yes	No

Is he your  ?

Is she your   ?

Unit 4 / People at Home

My father is tall and thin.

Let's Build

A. Practice the alphabet. CD 1 92

Gg
girl
garden

Gg
giraffe
giant

Hh
hat
house

Ii
ink
igloo

B. Listen and number. CD 1 93

Is he your father?
Yes, he is.

Is she your mother?
No, she isn't. She's my sister.

C. Practice.

"This is my sister. She's tall and pretty."

1. baby brother

2. father

3. grandfather

4. mother

5. grandmother

D. Talk about your family.

"My sister is tall and pretty."

Units 3-4 Listen and Review

A. Listen and circle.

1.
     a   b   c

2.
     a   b   c

3.
     a   b   c

4.
     a   b   c

B. Listen and number.

36   Units 3-4 Listen and Review

Let's Learn About Parts of the Body

A. Practice the words.

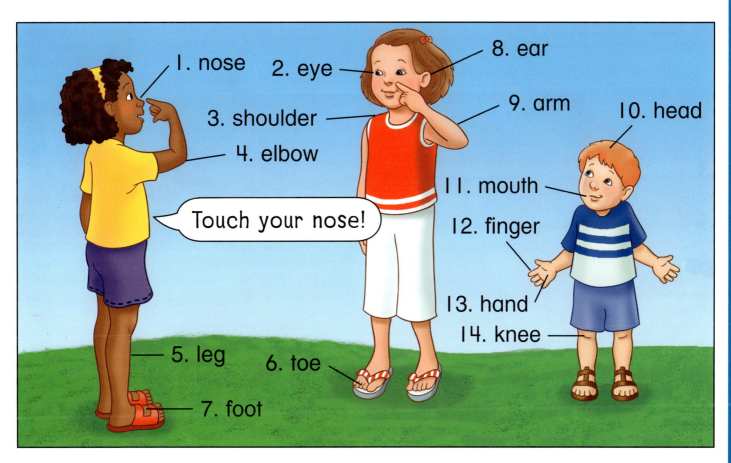

1. nose
2. eye
3. shoulder
4. elbow
5. leg
6. toe
7. foot
8. ear
9. arm
10. head
11. mouth
12. finger
13. hand
14. knee

Touch your nose!

Touch your nose!

B. Say these.

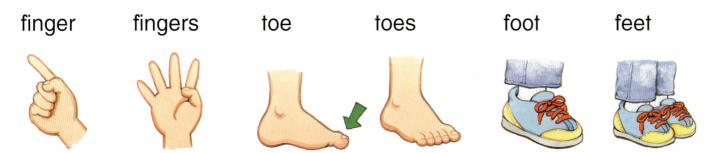

finger   fingers   toe   toes   foot   feet

Let's Learn About Parts of the Body   37

Unit 5 Birthday and Toys

 Let's Start

A. Let's talk.

How old are you?
I'm seven years old.

I am = I'm

B. Let's sing.

The Happy Birthday Song

It's my birthday today.
It's your birthday today.
It's my birthday today.
Happy birthday, Jenny!
One, two, three, four, five, six,
Seven years old!

Now I'm seven years old.
Now you're seven years old.
Now I'm seven years old.
Happy birthday, Jenny!

C. Let's move.

1. ride a bicycle

2. fly a kite

3. jump rope

4. play with a yo-yo

What can you do?
I can ride a bicycle.

Unit 5 / Birthday and Toys

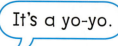

Let's Learn

A. Practice the words.

1. a yo-yo
2. a ball
3. a kite
4. a doll
5. a car
6. a robot
7. a bicycle
8. a jump rope
9. a puzzle
10. a bat

B. Practice the sentence.

It's a yo-yo.   It is = It's

C. Practice the question and answer.

What is it?
It's a doll.
I don't know.

do not = don't

D. Guess.
What is it?

Unit 5 / Birthday and Toys

Let's Learn More

A. Practice the words.

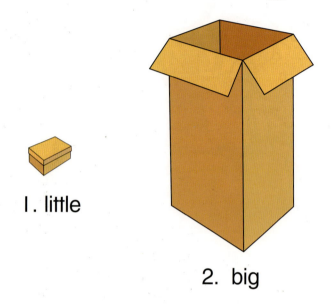

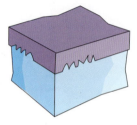

1. little
2. big
3. new
4. old

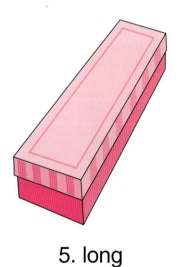

5. long
6. short
7. round
8. square

B. Practice the sentence.

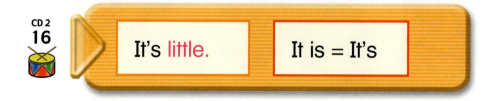

It's little.   It is = It's

Practice the question and answer.

Is it a round yo-yo?
　Yes, it is.
Is it a new doll?
　No, it isn't. It's an old doll.

is not = isn't
It is = It's

D. Listen and sing.

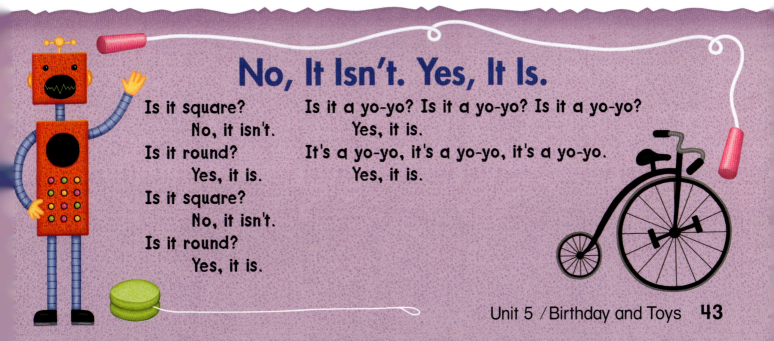

Unit 5 / Birthday and Toys

Let's Build

A. Practice the alphabet.

Jj	Kk	Ll	Mm

juice

jump rope

kite

kangaroo

lion

lemon

map

mother

B. Ask your partner.

What is it?
I don't know.
Is it a triangle?
No, it isn't.
Is it round?
No, it isn't.
Is it a star?
Yes, it is.

C. Ask and answer.

1.
2.
3.
4.

D. Listen and number.

Unit 5 / Birthday and Toys

Unit 6 Outdoors

Let's Start

A. Let's talk.

1. sunny   2. rainy   3. windy   4. cloudy   5. snowy

How's the weather?
It's sunny.

How is = How's
It is = It's

B. Let's sing.

How's the Weather?

How's the weather?
It's sunny.
How's the weather?
It's sunny.
How's the weather?
It's sunny. It's sunny today.

C. Let's move.

1. throw a ball

2. catch a ball

3. hit a ball

4. kick a ball

Can you throw a ball?
Yes, I can.
No, I can't.

cannot = can't

Unit 6 / Outdoors

Let's Learn

A. Practice the words.

1. a flower
2. flowers
3. a tree
4. trees

5. a cloud
6. clouds
7. a puddle
8. puddles

B. Practice the sentence.

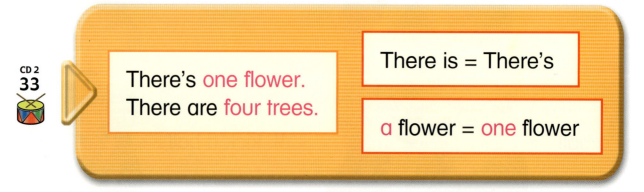

C. Let's count.

There is _____.   There are _____.

D. Practice the question and answer.

How many kites are there?
There is one kite.
How many trees are there?
There are eight trees.

Where's the bug? It's on the bag.

Let's Learn More

A. Practice the words.

1. in
2. on
3. under
4. by

B. Practice the sentence.

1. The bug is in the bag.

2. The bug is on the bag.

3. The bugs are under the bag.

4. The bugs are by the bag.

The bug **is in the bag.**
The bugs **are in the bag.**

C. Practice the question and answer.

Where's the doll?
It's under the table.
Where are the balls?
They're in the puddle.

Where is = Where's
They are = They're

D. Listen and sing.

Where Are the Bugs?

Where are the bugs?
They're on the flowers.
Where are the flowers?
They're by the tree.

Where's the tree?
It's in the puddle.
Where's the puddle?
It's under the tree.

Unit 6 / Outdoors

Let's Build

A. Practice the alphabet.

Nn nut, notebook
Oo octopus, omelet
Pp pencil, picture
Qq queen, question

B. Ask your partner.

Is there a doll in the bag? — Yes, there is.
Is there a doll in the bag? — No, there isn't.

52 Unit 6 / Outdoors

C. Ask and answer.

Are there bats in the bag?
   Yes, there are. No, there aren't.

D. Listen and circle.

There is one doll in the bag.

1.
   a   b

2.
   a   b

3.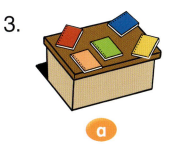
   a   b

4.
   a   b

Unit 6 / Outdoors   53

Units 5-6 Listen and Review

A. Listen and circle.

1.

a b c

2.
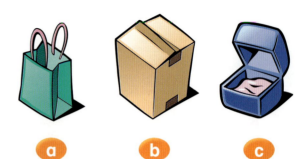
a b c

3.

a b c

4.

a b c

5.

a b c

6.

a b c

7.
a b c

8.
a b c

54 Units 5-6 Listen and Review

Let's Learn About Days of the Week

A. Ask and answer.

B. Practice.

Today is Monday.

Unit 7 Food

Let's Start

A. Let's talk.

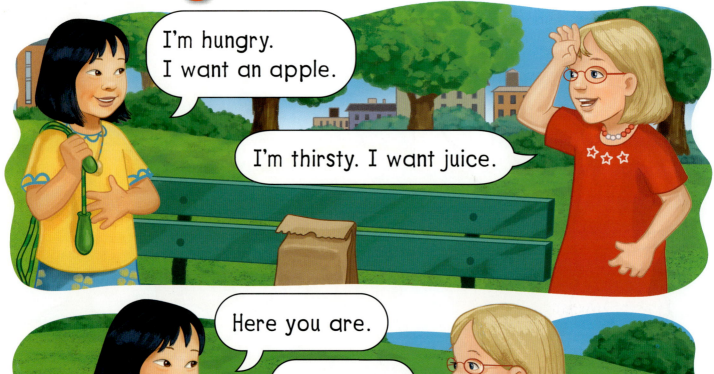

Here you are.
Thank you.
You're welcome.

You are = You're

B. Let's sing.

I Want An Apple

Apples, apples, where are the apples?
I'm hungry, I want an apple.
Apples, apples, where are the apples?
Here you are!
Thank you.
Thank you very much.
You're welcome.
Thank you very much.
You're welcome.
Thank you, thank you.
Thank you very much.
Thank you very much!
You're welcome!

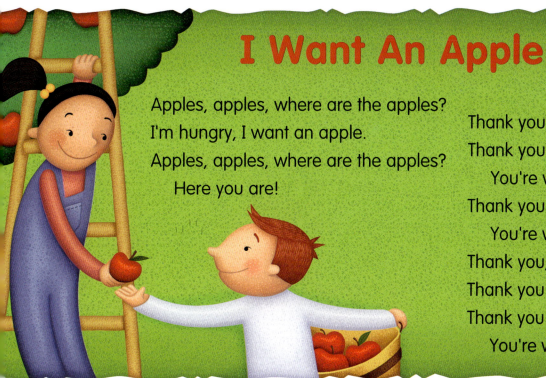

C. Let's move.

1. wash my hands

2. eat bread

3. drink milk

4. brush my teeth

I **wash my hands** every day.

What do you want?

I want an orange.

Let's Learn

A. Practice the words. CD 2 57

1. an orange

2. a banana

3. a soda

4. a milkshake

5. a cookie

6. a sandwich

7. an egg

8. a salad

B. Practice the sentence. CD 2 58

I want a banana.
I want an orange.

58   Unit 7 / Food

C. Practice the question and answer.

D. Listen and circle, then sing.

Let's Learn More

A. Practice the words. CD 2 · 64

1. chicken

2. fish

3. pizza

4. bread

5. rice

6. milk

7. cake

8. ice cream

B. Practice the sentence. CD 2 · 65

I want chicken.
I don't want fish.

do not = don't

60   Unit 7 / Food

C. Practice the question and answer.

Do you want cake?
Yes, I do.

Do you want rice?
No, I don't. I want milk.

D. Ask your partner.

Do you want fish?

Yes, I do.						
No, I don't.						

Let's Build

A. Practice the alphabet.

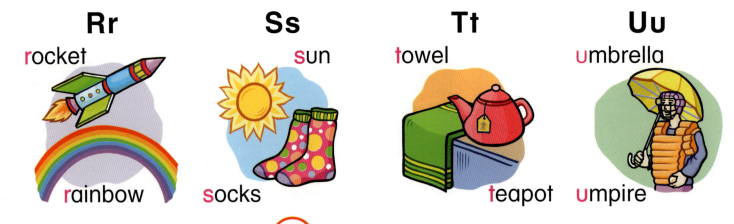

Rr rocket, rainbow

Ss sun, socks

Tt towel, teapot

Uu umbrella, umpire

B. Listen and circle.

I want a new car.

1. a b
2. a b
3. a b
4. a b

62 Unit 7 / Food

C. Ask your partner. Use the words.

1. big
2. thin
3. pretty
4. little
5. I don't know.

D. Ask and answer. Use the words.

1. big / little

2. old / new

3. green / blue

4. little / big

Unit 8 Animals

 **Let's Start**

A. Let's talk.

What's your favorite color?
Red.
I like blue.

What is = What's

B. Let's sing.

What's Your Favorite Color?

What's your favorite color, Ron?
My favorite color is red.
What's your favorite color, Pam?
My favorite color is pink.
What's your favorite color, Gus?
My favorite color is green.
What about you? What about you?
My favorite color is blue.

C. Let's move.

1. walk the dog

2. feed the turtle

3. brush the horse

4. pet the cat

I walk the dog every day.
I don't walk the dog every day.

do not = don't

Unit 8 / Animals 65

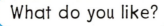 What do you like?

I like dogs.

Let's Learn

A. Practice the words.

1. a dog

2. dogs

3. a cat

4. cats

5. a bird

6. birds

7. a rabbit

8. rabbits

9. a turtle

10. turtles

11. a frog

12. frogs

B. Practice the sentence.

I like dogs.

66   Unit 8 / Animals

C. Practice the question and answer.

What do you like?
I like frogs.

D. Ask and answer.

What do you like?

	🐱	🐶	🐢	🐰	🐦	🐸
You						
Your partner						

Unit 8 / Animals

Do you like monkeys?

Yes, I do.

Let's Learn More

A. Practice the words.

1. a monkey
2. monkeys
3. a lion
4. lions

5. a tiger
6. tigers
7. a bear
8. bears

9. a giraffe
10. giraffes
11. an elephant
12. elephants

B. Practice the sentence.

I like monkeys.
I don't like bears.

do not = don't

Unit 8 / Animals

C. Practice the question and answer.

Do you like elephants?
　Yes, I do.
Do you like tigers?
　No, I don't.

do not = don't

Let's Build

A. Practice the alphabet.

Vv	Ww	Xx	Yy	Zz
vacuum	water	fox	yo-yo	zoo
van	wig	box	yarn	zebra

B. Ask your partner.

Do you like giraffes? — Yes, I do.

Do you like giraffes? — No, I don't.

70   Unit 8 / Animals

C. Ask and answer.

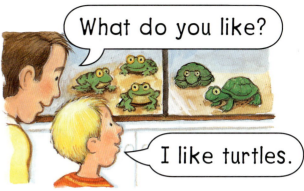

D. Listen and sing.

I Like Turtles

I like turtles.
What about you?
   I like turtles, too.
   I like turtles.
   I want a turtle.
      I want a turtle, too.

Units 7-8 Listen and Review

A. Listen and circle.

1.
   a   b   c

2.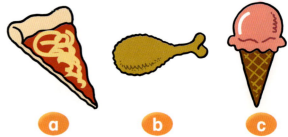
   a   b   c

3.
   a   b   c

4.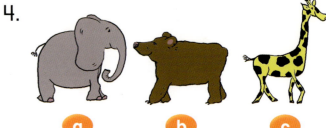
   a   b   c

5.
   a   b   c

6.
   a   b   c

B. Listen and number.

Let's Learn About Feelings

A. Ask and answer.

"Are you happy?"
"Yes, I am."
"No, I'm not."

1. happy
2. sad
3. angry
4. tired
5. sick
6. scared

B. Say these.

I'm _____.

1. hungry
2. thirsty
3. hot
4. cold

Let's Learn About Feelings 73

Let's Go 1 Syllabus

Unit 1   Things for School

Let's Start	**Let's Learn**	**Let's Learn More**	**Let's Build**
Hello, I'm Scott. What's your name? My name is Kate. *Introducing yourself* *Asking someone's name* Let's stand up. *Suggesting an activity*	It's a pencil. What's this? It's a pencil. *Identifying objects (singular)*	This is a globe. Is this a globe? Yes, it is. No, it isn't. *Asking about objects*	Is this your eraser? Yes, it is. No, it isn't. *Clarifying possession*

Unit 2   Colors and Shapes

Let's Start	**Let's Learn**	**Let's Learn More**	**Let's Build**
Hi, Andy. How are you? I'm fine. How are you? I'm fine. Thank you. *Greetings* Please take out your book. *Requests*	It's yellow. What color is this? It's green. It's red and blue. *Colors, identifying colors*	This is an oval. Is this a triangle? Yes, it is. No, it isn't. It's a star. *Shapes, identifying shapes*	What's this? It's a pen. What color is it? It's a red pen. *Describing objects with color and shape*

Units 1–2 Listen and Review	Let's Learn About Numbers 0–20 Counting

Unit 3   At the Store

Let's Start	**Let's Learn**	**Let's Learn More**	**Let's Build**
This is my friend, Sarah. Hello, Sarah. Hi. Let's play! *Introducing others* I can count to ten. *Describing abilities*	1 crayon, 10 crayons. How many crayons? 10 crayons. *Asking about numbers*	They're CDs. What's this? It's a CD. What are these? They're CDs. *Identifying objects (singular and plural)*	What color are these? They're pink. They're pink pencils. *Identifying characteristics of objects* *Contrasting singular and plural*

Unit 4   People at Home

Let's Start
Hi, Mom! I'm home.
This is my friend, John.
This is my mother.
It's nice to meet you.
Introducing family members

I can't find my book.
Describing abilities

Let's Learn
She's my grandmother.
He's my grandfather.

Who's she?
She's my grandmother.
Identifying and asking about people

Let's Learn More
This is a globe.

Is this a globe?
Yes, it is. No, it isn't.
Asking about objects

Let's Build
This is my sister.
She's tall and pretty.
My sister is tall and pretty.
Asking about and describing family members

Units 3–4 Listen and Review

Let's Learn About Parts of the Body
Touch your nose!

Unit 5   Birthday and Toys

Let's Start
Happy birthday, Jenny!
How old are you?
I'm seven years old.
Birthday greetings
Asking and telling age
This is for you.
Thank you.
Giving gifts
What can you do?
I can ride a bicycle.
Asking about abilities

Let's Learn
It's a yo-yo.

What is it?
It's a yo-yo.

Identifying objects

Let's Learn More
It's little. It's a little box.

Is it little?
Yes, it is.
No, it isn't. It's big.
Describing objects
Guessing

Let's Build
What is it? What are these? I don't know.
Are they pencils?
Are they blue? No, they aren't. Are they pens? Yes, they are.
Guessing based on size, shape, and color

Unit 6   Outdoors

Let's Start
How's the weather?
It's sunny
Asking about and describing weather
Can you throw a ball?
Yes, I can. No, I can't.
Asking about ability

Let's Learn
There is one flower.
There are four trees.

How many puddles are there?
There is one puddle.
How many flowers are there?
There are three flowers.
Counting
Describing a situation

Let's Learn More
The bug is in the desk.
The bugs are on the desk.

Where's the kite?
It's in the tree.

Where are the books?
They're under the table.
Asking about a location
Specifying location

Let's Build
Are there bats in the bag?
Yes, there are.
Identifying objects in a location
How many yo-yos are under the table?
Counting objects in a location

Let's Go 1 Syllabus

| Units 5–6 Listen and Review | Let's Learn About Days of the Week
What day is it today?
Today is Monday |

Unit 7   Food

Let's Start	Let's Learn	Let's Learn More	Let's Build
I'm hungry. I want an apple. *Expressing hunger and thirst* Here you are. 　Thank you. You're welcome. *Giving and receiving* I wash my hands everyday. *Describing everyday activities*	What do you want? I want an orange. *Asking what someone wants*	I want chicken. I don't want fish. Do you want chicken? Yes, I do. No, I don't. *Expressing wants*	Do you want a big robot? No, I don't. I want a new computer. *Expressing wants with descriptive adjectives*

Unit 8   Animals

Let's Start	Let's Learn	Let's Learn More	Let's Build
What's your favorite color? Red. What about you? I like blue. *Asking about favorites* I don't walk the dog every day. *Describing everyday activities*	I like dogs. What do you like? I like frogs. *Asking about likes*	Do you like lions? Yes, I do. No, I don't. I like monkeys. I don't like tigers. *Asking and telling about likes and dislikes*	What do you like? I like sandwiches. What do you want? I want a sandwich. *Contrasting wants and likes*

| Units 7–8 Listen and Review | Let's Learn About Feelings
Are you happy?
Yes, I am. No, I'm not. |

Teacher and Student Card List Level One

1. stand up
2. sit down
3. make a circle
4. make a line
5. a pencil
6. a pen
7. a bag
8. a book
9. a desk
10. a chair
11. a ruler
12. an eraser
13. a map
14. a marker
15. a globe
16. a table
17. a board
18. a wastebasket
19. a poster
20. a crayon
21. fine
22. great
23. OK
24. take out your book
25. put away your book
26. draw a picture
27. point to the poster
28. yellow
29. blue
30. red
31. green
32. orange
33. purple
34. pink
35. brown
36. black
37. white
38. gray
39. a triangle
40. a square
41. a circle
42. a star
43. a heart
44. a rectangle
45. an oval
46. a diamond
47. ant
48. apple
49. box
50. bug
51. cat
52. computer
53. circle
54. circus
55. zero
56. one
57. two
58. three
59. four
60. five
61. six
62. seven
63. eight
64. nine
65. ten
66. eleven
67. twelve
68. thirteen
69. fourteen
70. fifteen
71. sixteen
72. seventeen
73. eighteen
74. nineteen
75. twenty
76. count to ten
77. write the word
78. read a book
79. say the alphabet
80. a crayon
81. crayons
82. a marker
83. markers
84. a notebook
85. notebooks
86. a pencil case
87. pencil cases
88. a CD
89. CDs
90. a video game
91. video games
92. a cell phone
93. cell phones
94. a computer
95. computers
96. dog
97. diamond
98. elephant
99. egg
100. five
101. fish
102. find my book
103. reach the bookshelf
104. see the board
105. hear the teacher
106. grandmother
107. mother
108. sister
109. baby sister
110. grandfather
111. father
112. brother
113. tall
114. short
115. young
116. old
117. pretty
118. ugly
119. fat
120. thin
121. girl
122. garden
123. giraffe
124. giant
125. hat
126. house
127. igloo
128. ink
129. eye
130. nose
131. mouth
132. ear
133. finger
134. fingers
135. hand
136. toe
137. toes
138. foot
139. feet
140. head
141. shoulder
142. arm
143. elbow
144. leg
145. knee
146. ride a bicycle
147. fly a kite
148. jump rope
149. play with a yo-yo
150. a yo-yo
151. a ball
152. a kite
153. a doll
154. a car
155. a robot
156. a bicycle
157. a jump rope
158. a puzzle
159. a bat
160. little
161. big
162. new
163. old
164. long
165. short
166. round
167. square
168. jump rope
169. juice
170. kangaroo
171. kite
172. lemon
173. lion
174. map
175. mother
176. sunny
177. rainy
178. windy
179. cloudy
180. snowy
181. throw a ball
182. catch a ball
183. hit a ball
184. kick a ball
185. a flower
186. flowers
187. a tree
188. trees
189. a cloud
190. clouds
191. a puddle
192. puddles
193. in
194. on
195. under
196. by
197. nut
198. notebook
199. octopus
200. omelet
201. pencil
202. picture
203. queen
204. question
205. Sunday
206. Monday
207. Tuesday
208. Wednesday
209. Thursday
210. Friday
211. Saturday
212. wash my hands
213. eat bread
214. drink milk
215. brush my teeth
216. an orange
217. a banana
218. a soda
219. a milkshake
220. a cookie
221. a sandwich
222. an egg
223. a salad
224. chicken
225. fish
226. pizza
227. bread
228. rice
229. milk
230. cake
231. ice cream
232. rocket
233. rainbow
234. socks
235. sun
236. teapot
237. towel
238. umbrella
239. umpire
240. walk the dog
241. feed the turtle
242. pet the cat
243. brush the horse
244. a dog
245. dogs
246. a cat
247. cats
248. a bird
249. birds
250. a rabbit
251. rabbits
252. a turtle
253. turtles
254. a frog
255. frogs
256. a monkey
257. monkeys
258. a lion
259. lions
260. a tiger
261. tigers
262. a bear
263. bears
264. a giraffe
265. giraffes
266. an elephant
267. elephants
268. vacuum
269. van
270. water
271. wig
272. box
273. fox
274. yarn
275. yo-yo
276. zebra
277. zoo
278. happy
279. sad
280. angry
281. tired
282. sick
283. scared
284. hungry
285. thirsty
286. hot
287. cold

Word List

A
angry 73
ant 16
apple 16
arm 37

B
baby sister 30
bag 4
ball 40
banana 58
bat 40
bear 68
bicycle 40
big 42
bird 68
black 12
blue 12
board 6
book 4
box 16
bread 60
brother 30
brown 12
brush my teeth 57
brush the horse 65
bug 16
by 50

C
cake 60
car 40
cat 66
catch a ball 47
CD 24
cell phone 24
chair 4
chicken 60
circle 14
circus 16
cloud 48
cloudy 46
cold 73
computer 24
cookie 58
count to ten 21
crayon 6

D
desk 4
diamond 14
dog 66
doll 40
draw a picture 11
drink milk 57

E
ear 37
eat bread 57
egg 58
eight 19
eighteen 19
elbow 37
elephant 68
eleven 19
eraser 4
eye 37

F
fat 32
father 30
feed the turtle 65
feet 37
fifteen 19
find my book 29
fine 11
finger 37
fish 26, 60
five 19
flower 48
fly a kite 39
foot 37
four 19
fourteen 19
fox 70
Friday 55
frog 66

G
garden 34
giant 34
giraffe 68
girl 34
globe 6
grandfather 30
grandmother 30
gray 12

great 11
green 12

H
hand 37
happy 73
hat 34
head 37
hear the teacher 29
heart 14
hit a ball 47
hot 73
house 34
hungry 73

I
ice cream 60
igloo 34
in 50
ink 34

J
juice 44
jump rope 40
jump 39

K
kangaroo 44
kick a ball 47
kite 40
knee 37

L
leg 37
lemon 44
lion 68
little 42
long 42

M
make a circle 3
make a line 3
map 6
marker 6
milk 60
milkshake 58
Monday 55
monkey 68

mother 30
mouth 37

N
new 42
nine 19
nineteen 19
nose 37
notebook 22
nut 52

O
octopus 52
OK 11
old 32
omelet 52
on 50
one 19
orange 12, 58
oval 14

P
pen 4
pencil 4
pencil case 22
pet the cat 65
picture 52
pink 12
pizza 60
play with a yo-yo 39
point to the poster 11
poster 6
pretty 32
puddle 48
purple 12
put away your book 11
puzzle 40

Q
queen 52
question 52

R
rabbit 66
rainbow 62

rainy 46
reach the bookshelf 29
read a book 21
rectangle 14
red 12
rice 60
ride a bicycle 39
robot 40
rocket 62
rope 39
round 42
ruler 4

S
sad 73
salad 58
sandwich 58
Saturday 55
say the alphabet 21
scared 73
see the board 29
seven 19
seventeen 19
short 32
shoulder 37
sick 73
sister 30
sit down 3
six 19
sixteen 19
snowy 46
socks 62
soda 58
square 14
stand up 3
star 14
sun 62
Sunday 55
sunny 46

T
table 6
take out your book 11
tall 32
teapot 62
ten 19
thin 32
thirsty 73

thirteen 19
three 19
throw a ball 47
Thursday 55
tiger 68
tired 73
toe 37
towel 62
tree 48
triangle 14
Tuesday 55
turtle 66
twelve 19
twenty 19
two 19

U
ugly 32
umbrella 62
umpire 62
under 50

V
vacuum 70
van 70
video game 24

W
walk the dog 65
wash my hands 57
wastebasket 6
water 70
Wednesday 55
white 12
wig 70
windy 46
write the word 21

Y
yarn 70
yellow 12
young 32
yo-yo 40

Z
zebra 70
zero 19
zoo 70